RAF Tangmere

IN OLD PHOTOGRAPHS

GW00643438

ROYAL AIR FORCE STATION
TANGMERE

ATTACK TO DEFEND

RAF Tangmere

IN OLD PHOTOGRAPHS

Collected by ANDY SAUNDERS

Alan Sutton Publishing Limited
Phoenix Mill · Far Thrupp
Stroud · Gloucestershire

First published 1992

Front Cover Illustration: Pilots and Hurricanes of 601 Squadron

For Jimmy (J. Beedle, 1920 to 1989) my good friend and co-founder of Tangmere Military Aviation Museum

British Library Cataloguing in Publication Data

Saunders, Andy
RAF Tangmere in Old Photographs
I. Title
358.417094225

ISBN 0–7509–172–1

Typeset in 9/10 Sabon.
Typesetting and origination by
Alan Sutton Publishing.
Printed and bound by
WBC, Bridgend, Mid Glam.

Contents

Introduction

Royal Air Force Tangmere was one of the most famous stations in the history of the Service; it was also one of the finest. Today the aircraft have long since gone; its buildings have all but totally yielded to developers' bulldozers. The weed-choked runways are partially ripped up, greenhouses sprawl where once Hurricanes and Spitfires sat awaiting action and the control tower now languishes in a sad state of dereliction.

Tangmere as a flying field owes its origins to a minor flying mishap on 19 November 1916, when Flt. Lt. Geoffrey Dorman was forced to make an emergency landing in his FE2b while *en route* from Gosport to Shoreham. Landing in a large field at what was then Bayley's Farm, Dorman's machine tipped up on the rough ground and suffered a broken propeller. Writing his report of the episode, Dorman noted that the site would make an excellent location for an aerodrome. The rest, as they say, is history. It is that particular piece of history I have told here through photographs, tracing Tangmere's long and illustrious associations with the RAF.

It was not until 1917 that work on the site began, with much of the labour supplied by German prisoners of war. By March of the following year, 91, 92 and 93 Squadrons of the Royal Flying Corps moved in for training prior to transfer to France and the Western Front. The aircraft then in use at Tangmere were a selection of Avro 504s, SE5As, Sopwith Pups and Sopwith Dolphins. The first Station Commander was Maj. W.V. Strugnell MC. At this time the station was under construction and canvas Bessonau-type hangars were in use, pending completion of the massive General Service or Belfast hangars. A spur railway line was laid from the main line at Oving in order to bring in building materials and supplies. The face of Tangmere was changing for ever, and George Bayley's Church Farm was vanishing rapidly. However, the War Office planners had other ideas for Tangmere: it was intended that, on completion, the place would be handed to the United States Army Air Service (USAS) as a training depot station for the huge Handley Page 0/400 aircraft. Delays in the completion of the buildings and in the delivery of the aeroplanes meant that events rather overtook the planners. It was not until six days after the Armistice had been signed that the USAS actually moved in with a few BE2Es, Farmans and DeHavilland 4s. It is believed that none of the 0/400s actually arrived before the Americans departed, leaving Tangmere in the hands of the embryonic RAF, formed just eight months previously out of the RFC. Very soon, Tangmere would become redundant, reduced to a holding station for units returning from the Continent. The Air Ministry, however, retained ownership of the site when the station closed in 1920. Then in 1923, a certain Mr Bentley had his eye on Tangmere as a site for a car factory to build his now famous cars. He planned to build test tracks across what was then just a large field; the hard runways were a much later feature of Tangmere's development. He decided not to buy, however, and in 1925 Tangmere re-opened as the Coastal Area Storage Unit. The domestic site was enlarged with new brick buildings, including Officers', NCOs' and Airmen's Messes, barrack blocks, Station HQ, NAAFI, Sick Bay, Guardroom and parade ground. Obviously, the RAF had long-term plans for Tangmere. Indeed, the CASU was replaced in November 1926, when 43 Squadron moved in with its Gamecock fighters, followed not long after by 1 Squadron with its Armstrong Whitworth Siskin IIIAs. This was the start of a long-standing association between Tangmere and the two squadrons who both came to regard the place as their ancestral home.

The 1920s and '30s at Tangmere can be considered the aerodrome's halcyon days, and the station, its aircraft, personnel and achievements became a symbol of excellence in the RAF. Postings here were much sought after. Throughout the summer all flying was concentrated between 7 a.m. and 1 p.m., leaving the rest of the day free for leisure pursuits. During those years the silver biplanes of 1 Squadron and 43 Squadron sported red bands and chequerboard markings respectively. They vied with each other for superiority, both squadrons regularly displaying aerobatic and formation flying skills at air displays. Each year on Empire Air Day, Tangmere opened its gates for thrilling displays, and the Auxiliary Air Force squadrons all hoped that summer camp would be at Tangmere. But then in the late 1930s, war clouds were gathering. More building development and the formation of two new fighter squadrons at Tangmere (72 and 87) signalled an expansion programme, and 217 Coastal Reconnaisance Squadron, equipped with Ansons, moved in. An asphalt perimeter track was also constructed. By September 1938 the silver Hawker Fury biplanes had been camouflaged brown and green, air-raid shelters had been dug and the station had effectively been put on a 'war footing'. Tangmere would never be the same again.

By the time war came one year later, the biplanes had been replaced with Hawker Hurricanes, although 1 and 43 Squadrons were still in residence. Within a few days, however, 1 Squadron had been despatched to France where it fought hard and with distinction.

The next five years were the busiest and most important in the history of RAF Tangmere and it would be impossible here to describe fully the comings and goings of squadrons and personnel, or of events and personalities making history at Tangmere during 1939–45. Some, though, are worthy of mention and undoubtedly Tangmere's moment of crowning glory was during the Battle of Britain. During that period in 1940, Tangmere's squadrons (and those of its satellite, Westhampnett) acquitted themselves admirably. Success, though, was tempered with loss, and testimony to the ferocity of the struggle are rows of war graves in Tangmere churchyard, side-by-side with former enemies.

One particularly harrowing day was 16 August 1940, when Tangmere was subjected to an attack by Junkers 87 Stuka dive bombers which left the aerodrome battered but still operational. All the same, one hangar was burned out, two more damaged beyond repair, the 'garage' hangar roof had collapsed and dozens of other buildings were left in a ruinous shambles. Thirteen died, twenty were seriously injured, and three Blenheims, seven Hurricanes, one Spitfire and one Magister were destroyed with many other aircraft damaged. Despite this state of affairs, the Operational Record Book for Tangmere stated: 'The depressing situation was dealt with in an orderly manner and it is considered that the traditions of the RAF were upheld by all ranks. It must be considered that the major attack launched on this station was a victory for the RAF.' If it is stretching the imagination a little to consider this attack in any way a 'victory' for the RAF, it is fact that the attackers were dealt a severe mauling by Tangmere's resident fighter squadrons.

Throughout the Battle of Britain and beyond, Tangmere was a key Sector Station in 11 Group, Fighter Command. However, as the RAF went onto the offensive, its role changed from defence to offence while maintaining an important place in the air defence of the UK. From 1941, Tangmere became home to the Tangmere Wing of three Spitfire squadrons, led in the first instance by the legendary Wg. Cdr. Douglas Bader. Then in August of the same year, Bader was lost over France and taken as a prisoner of war. One year later, in August 1942, Tangmere was to play a key part in the Dieppe operation. Its fighter squadrons participated in what was then the greatest single air battle of all time.

Throughout all the terror of war, life at Tangmere retained something of its pre-war relaxed gaiety, albeit overshadowed by a deadly and earnest intent. Entertainment played a key part in the war effort through its morale-boosting effect on frayed and jangled nerves. Vera Lynn, Noel Coward and Vivien Leigh were among the top names who appeared in the 'Tangmere Theatre', and in February 1943 the company of the Windmill Theatre gave performances for station personnel. Distinguished visitors, too, were often at Tangmere. King George VI and Queen Elizabeth, the Duke of Kent, the Duchess of Gloucester, General De Gaulle, Anthony Eden, Lord Mountbatten, Sir Archibald Sinclair, Viscount Trenchard, Air Chief Marshall Sir Hugh Dowding, Field Marshall Montgomery and General Eisenhower were all at one time visitors.

Perhaps the most notable work carried out from Tangmere was that by the Lysanders of 161 Squadron, which used the aerodrome as a forward operations base for taking agents in and out of occupied France. These clandestine missions were flown under cover of darkness and amid great secrecy. Tangmere Cottage, just across the road from the main gate to the camp, was used as an HQ building for these secret flights and the agents were brought here to prepare for the flight out. A hazardous undertaking, these missions resulted in surprisingly few casualties, despite landings at night in farmers' fields under the very noses of the Germans and with only torches to guide the pilots in. From Tangmere, the agents who assassinated the notorious Reinhard Heydrich parachuted into Czechoslovakia from a Halifax bomber. The operation succeeded, but resulted in reprisals against two Czech villages.

The courage of these pilots was unequalled in the history of the RAF, and yet they would modestly only describe themselves as 'taxi drivers', reserving any plaudits for courage for the brave agents they delivered and collected.

It was such agents, of course, who helped lay the foundations for a successful invasion of Europe. When D-Day came on 6 June 1944, Tangmere played a major role once more by providing key elements in the fighter 'umbrella' over beaches and bridgeheads, but thereafter anticlimax was the order of the day.

Tangmere became a quiet backwater, but at the cessation of hostilities its fighters had accounted for 811 enemy aircraft destroyed, 245 probably destroyed and 432 damaged. By any standards, this was an impressive tally for a fighter station.

In 1945 the Fighter Leaders School came to Tangmere, as well as the Enemy Aircraft Flight and the Naval Air Fighting Development Unit. Together these units flew an exotic collection of aircraft types ranging from Spitfires, Mustangs, Tempests, Barracudas, Avengers and the Grumman Tigercat, to the captured Messerschmitts, Heinkels and Junkers of the Enemy Aircraft Flight.

In the immediate post-war period, a refurbishment programme saw the replacement of the Belfast hangars with three T2 hangars, all of the original Belfasts having succumbed to bomb, storm and accident. In September 1946, however, the name of Tangmere was put firmly back on the aviation map with the formation of the Meteor-equipped High Speed Flight. Its three pilots, Gp. Capt. E.M. Donaldson, Sqn. Ldr. W.A. Waterton and Flt. Lt. N. Duke made an attempt on the World Air Speed Record. At a speed of 616 mph (991 km/h), the record was broken by Donaldson off the Sussex coast. The actual record-breaking Meteor is preserved at Tangmere Military Aviation Museum.

As Tangmere moved into the jet age, the pre-war residents, Squadrons 1 and 43, were to return with Meteors. But during the 'Meteor period' other squadrons equipped with the type were also resident, including Squadrons 29, 222 and 226. For a time, silver aeroplanes marked with the familiar colourful pre-war squadron markings were to grace the skies of Sussex. Then in 1953 another colourful and exciting aeroplane appeared at Tangmere – the crimson Hawker Hunter prototype. In this aeroplane, Sqn. Ldr. Neville Duke raised the World Air Speed Record to 727.63 mph (1,171 km/h) on 7 September. Duke had been part of the earlier 1946 High Speed Flight, but was not the record-breaking pilot at that time. The Hunter used, WB188, is also displayed at Tangmere Military Aviation Museum.

In that same year, Her Majesty The Queen approved the design for Tangmere's own badge. Its motto, 'Attack to Defend', reflected past glories, but in truth Tangmere was now in its twilight years as a premier station. A portent of demise was, perhaps, the posting of 43 Squadron to a new home in Scotland. But with the Hunter era dawning, Tangmere had one last spell of glory when 34 Squadron formed with Hunters in 1954, followed shortly by the re-equipping of 1 Squadron who were then still resident. In 1956 both squadrons were posted to Cyprus to take part in the abortive Suez Campaign, later to return to their home base. By 1958, however, Tangmere's role as a frontline fighter station was over and the base transferred from Fighter Command to 90 (Signals) Group, Signals Command, who operated Varsities of 115 Squadron and Canberras of 245 Squadron. Both units served in the calibration and checking of radar and navigational equipment. The yellow Air Sea Rescue Whirlwind helicopters of 22 Squadron added a little colour and variety at this time, but the writing was on the wall (or, rather, on Air Ministry desks!) so far as Tangmere's future was concerned. In 1963 the Canberras and Varsities were transferred to RAF Watton, Suffolk. Then in 1964 the station transferred to Transport Command, 38 Group Support Unit, which was the non-flying support unit for 38 Group's mobile forces. An army unit (244 Signals Squadron) formed part of 38 Group Support Unit at Tangmere, but with the departure of 22 Squadron's Whirlwinds to nearby RAF Thorney Island in 1964, the end was nigh. In its final years, Tactical Signals Units, the Joint Services Language School and 623 Gliding School maintained a presence, and the odd Hercules of 242 Operational Conversion Unit, Thorney Island, used the airfield for cargo parachute training drops.

Tangmere was again in the news when Flt. Lt. Alan Pollock took off from the aifrield in his 1 Squadron Hunter on 4 April 1968, after taking part in local celebrations to mark the 50th anniversary of the RAF. Before returning to his home base (West Raynham), Pollock carried out a low-level beat up of Westminster, then proceeded to fly down the Thames and under the top span of Tower Bridge. The incident earned Pollock an early retirement from the RAF and captured world headlines. It was to be Tangmere's infamous swan-song, for on 16 October 1970 the station finally closed.

The RAF ensign was hauled down for the last time and a farewell parade saw local and civic dignitaries mixing with Tangmere personnel, many veterans and old-timers coming back for the sad farewell. Then, after the Spitfire gate guardian had been hauled away as if to signal the final death throes, the 'corpse' was left to slowly rot. For a while the station languished under a 'Care and Maintenance' order, and 623 GS remained until June 1975. In 1979, however, the final blow fell in the form of the auctioneer's hammer. Most of the flying field returned to agriculture, though not to the Bayley family. The buildings, meanwhile, were sold for development, with the exception of the hangars and control tower. The latter, in a state of utter dereliction, is now the property of the Church Commissioners, while the hangars were put into service as grain stores for the EEC Agricultural Intervention Board. For a while the concrete runways, peri-tracks and aprons were used for Fire Brigade and Police driver training. The last links with a military past lingered on a little longer in the form of a Royal Navy communications unit in a small compound and a Military Police Training Facility. Then, almost in a *coup de grâce*, the SAS blew holes in the Officer's Mess walls during anti-terrorist training exercises. The end had finally and ignominiously come.

A memorial stone in the village and the Tangmere Military Aviation Museum keep alive the memories of Tangmere's past and, as one poet wrote:

> This field as famed as Agincourt
> Or Crécy, with their mailed hosts,
> Where those who valued freedom fought,
> Stands guarded by its valiant ghosts.

Indeed, if there are ghosts, they are surely here!

Andy Saunders 1992

SECTION ONE

The Birth of RAF Tangmere

A BE2e aeroplane, 1917. The hangars in the background are under construction. German POW labour was used during the building work. Note the discarded luggage label in the foreground; perhaps it reads 'Destination France'?

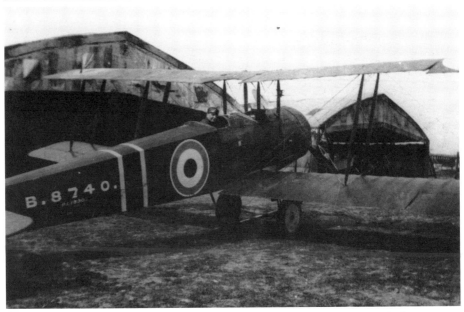

An Avro 504, with 2nd Lt. Wilson of 92 Squadron seated in the cockpit. The hangars are of the temporary 'Bessonau' canvas type.

This Avro 504 had a landing mishap, ending up in the building site a trifle the worse for wear but with its pilot unharmed.

2nd Lt. E. Wilson and a Sopwith Dolphin in front of the canvas hangars, 1918.

2nd Lt. E. Wilson, 92 Squadron, 1918. This was just prior to the date when the Royal Flying Corps, with their army uniforms and ranks, became the Royal Air Force. Behind Lt. Wilson is the railway track which was a spur line from Oving. This brought building materials and supplies directly onto the aerodrome.

Maj. W.V. Strugnell MC in an SE5A. He was appointed as the first Station Commander at Tangmere in March 1918.

Maj. Conningham DSO MC prepares to lead 92 Squadron from Tangmere to France, summer 1918. He is seated in an SE5A, D6883, the aeroplane in which he scored at least three of his confirmed victories over the Western Front.

Although indistinct, this captures a significant moment in the history of Tangmere, July 1918. Maj. Conningham leads 92 Squadron off to France in their SE5As. Note the waiting ambulance and one of the officer's ladies with her parasol. The main hangars are almost complete, but a canvas Bessonau-type hangar may be seen in the foreground.

A heavy landing resulted in this rather lop-sided machine at Tangmere, summer 1918.

One of the first of many tragic flying accidents throughout Tangmere's history occurred when this Sopwith Dolphin crashed just outside the aerodrome's southern boundary, 27 July 1918. Lt. George Lipsett of 91 Squadron was killed.

SECTION TWO

Tangmere's Halcyon Years 1925–38

Sqn. Ldr. A.F. Brooke with his Gloster Gamecock of 43 Squadron, soon after the station reopened in 1926. Note the black-and-white check streamers tied to the wing struts – the colours of 43 Squadron.

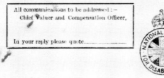

All communications to be addressed :—
Chief Valuer and Compensation Officer.

In your reply please quote.............................

DIRECTORATE OF LANDS,

THE WAR OFFICE, DISPOSAL AND LIQUIDATION
COMMISSION AND AIR MINISTRY,

CAXTON HOUSE WEST,

TOTHILL STREET, S.W.1.

443353/23.
454646/23. (D.L.3.b.)   9th October, 1923.

Dear Sir,

Tangmere Aerodrome.

With reference to the temporary occupation
by the Royal Air Force of a portion of your land at
this Aerodrome, I am proposing to come down to see
you on Monday next with a view to discussing the
compensation to be paid for such occupation, and should
be glad to know if it would be convenient for me to
see you at your farm on that day.

I am to say that the Air Ministry are
proposing to re-open the Aerodrome as a permanent
station and I enclose a plan showing the land in your
occupation coloured purple and green, which it is
proposed to acquire, and I should be glad when seeing
you to discuss also, arrangements with regard to your
future cultivation of this land with a view to your
seeding the same down to grass next Spring, subject of
course to our agreeing terms with the respective Owners
for the purchase of the same.

Yours faithfully,

Captain,
for Deputy Chief Valuer and
Compensation Officer.

G. Bayley, Esq.,
    Church Farm,
        Tangmere,
            Nr. Chichester,
                Sussex.

This 1923 letter to farmer George Bayley set the scene for the requisition of land and the
re-opening of RAF Tangmere in 1925.

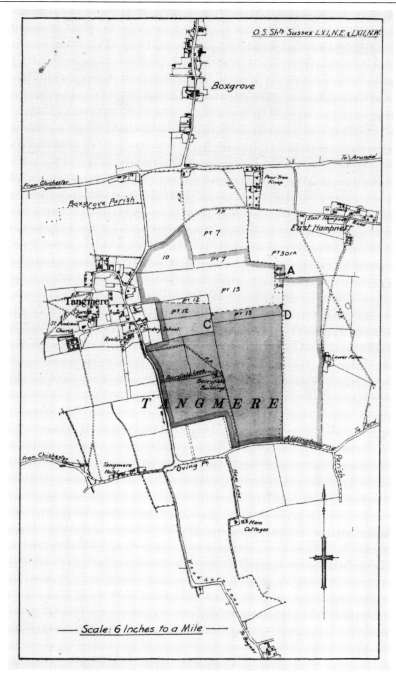

Tangmere site plan, 1923. Other drawings noted depressions to be filled, trees to be felled and telegraph wires to be removed.

By the late 1920s, Tangmere had become a permanent home station for RAF fighter squadrons. Nestling beneath the South Downs, this almost idyllic setting was a popular posting. This view is looking northwards.

Aerial view of Tangmere Aerodrome, 1920s. This shows the main building and domestic site, dominated by the huge General Service or Belfast hangars. Note the black circles (top left), which are the landing wheels of an aeroplane formating on the photographer's aircraft.

One of 43 Squadron's Tangmere-based Gloster Gamecocks of the 1926–1928 period. This may be somewhere other than Tangmere, as the buildings seem unfamiliar.

The officers and men of 43 Squadron in front of the NAAFI Institute at Tangmere, 1929. Now converted into flats, this building is almost the last to survive on the original aerodrome site.

An Armstrong Whitworth Siskin fighter of 43 Squadron, *c.* 1928. Seen from the inside, the massive trussed hangar with its lattice-work roof construction dwarfs this diminutive but delightful aircraft.

A landing mishap left this Siskin of 43 Squadron stranded without its wheels in the middle of the flying field. The walk back to the Flight Hut for a shaken pilot trying to work out what he was going to tell the CO must have seemed a very long way!

DeHavilland DH9As of 600 (City of London) Squadron, Auxiliary Air Force, airborne from Tangmere on summer camp, August 1928.

Armstrong Whitworth Siskin fighters of 43 Squadron in formation over the Sussex countryside, 1930. It was in this year that the squadron performed the first tied-together aerobatics.

Another mishap resulted in this Siskin, J9903, of 1 Squadron, flipping over onto its back and becoming another candidate for repair.

This 1 Squadron Siskin, J9887, suffered a landing mishap at Tangmere, 1929. Motor transport has just arrived to tow the aeroplane back to the hangars for inspection and possible repair. Incidents such as this were relatively common-place.

This 43 Squadron Siskin, J9359, collided at 3,000 ft near Chichester with the Hawker Hornet prototype during comparative trials, 11 April 1930. The Siskin pilot, FO Herber-Percy, baled out safely.

This was all that remained of the Hawker Hornet, J9682, after the accident. Its pilot, FO Brake of 1 Squadron, also baled out and broke an arm on hitting the tailplane. The Hornet was the forerunner of the famous Hawker Fury fighter, soon to equip Tangmere's squadrons.

A brand new and unnumbered Bristol Bulldog fighter visits Tangmere, 1928. Although this type never equipped Tangmere-based squadrons, it is believed that pilots of 1 and 43 Squadrons flew this aeroplane during its visit. On 30 September 1930, three Bulldogs of 17 Squadron, at Tangmere for air exercises, crashed into trees at Arundel Park. Two pilots died and the third was injured.

DeHavilland DH 60M Moth of the Central Flying School visiting Tangmere, 1930. On 23 April 1931 an aircraft of this type crashed at Bury Hill, Sussex, after colliding with a 43 Squadron Siskin. The occupants of the Moth, Air Vice Marshal Vesey-Holt CMG DSO and Flt. Lt. Moody MC, were both killed. The Siskin pilot, Sgt. Wareham, flew safely back to Tangmere.

An unusual visitor to Tangmere was this one-off Hawker Hart, May 1931. It was built as a private venture testbed. Its Armstrong Siddeley Panther engine makes an ungainly contrast to the sleek-cowled Kestrel engine of the Fury.

The one-off Jupiter engined Hawker Hawkfinch, J8776, visits Tangmere, 1928. It was originally envisaged as a replacement for the Siskin and Gamecock, but in the end only one was ever built.

A sleek, silver Hawker Fury in the squadron hangar against the lattice-framed door. During 1931 these replaced the Siskins of 43 Squadron.

A few weeks later the same Hawker Fury aeroplane sports 43 Squadron's chequerboard markings on its tailfin in addition to the distinctive wing and fuselage markings. However, it ignominiously ended up in this landing accident, March 1937. As usual the incident attracts onlookers.

Hawker Furies of 43 Squadron in formation over Sussex, 1931. The glorious countryside, brilliant summers and gaily marked aeroplanes belied the warlike intent of the machines, for which RAF Station Tangmere was built. 'It seemed', said one who was there, 'the best flying club ever, situated at the best country club in the world.' How soon it would all change.

On parade! The Hawker Fury biplanes of Tangmere's resident Squadrons, 1 and 43, line up for an inspection by the AOC. The white hut is the Flying Control Office, for this was before the days of Air Traffic Control and control towers. 'All Pilots Report Here', commands the notice over the door.

'A good landing', so the saying goes, 'is one you can walk away from.' This incident was the result of PO Rory Chisholm's 'wings' qualification flight at Tangmere with 604 Squadron, 28 July 1931. With none other than the AOC, Air Commodore McNeece-Foster, as passenger, Chisholm crashed his Wapiti on landing and his superior was catapulted from the wreckage. Fortunately, the only casualties were Chisholm's pride and the Air Commodore's dignity – Chisholm walked away unhurt and *still* gained his wings!

Airmen photographers of 604 Squadron hard at work during summer camp, 1931. In the foreground the remnants of fabric from Chisholm's Wapiti provide a useful sun bed.

What the well-dressed airman-photographer of 604 Squadron was wearing at Tangmere in 1929.

604 (Bomber) Squadron, Auxiliary Air Force, summer camp, 1933. The tall officer (centre rear) is FO Michael Doulton of the Doulton porcelain family. He was later killed in the Battle of Britain.

The entire photographic section of 604 Squadron at Tangmere annual camp, August 1933. Note the uncomfortable, high-necked collars and puttees. The airman seated at front left seems not to have yet mastered the art of puttee application.

The Westland Wapitis of 604 Squadron, Auxiliary Air Force, in formation over Tangmere, 1933. The white chalk circle with its letter L was the landing circle. Runways were a future development.

Hawker Furies belonging to 1 Squadron, the other fighter squadron resident at Tangmere throughout the pre-war years. By contrast with 43 Squadron's chequerboard design, the aeroplanes of 1 Squadron sported red bar markings. Both squadrons vied with each other in friendly rivalry for overall excellence during their long association with Tangmere.

The pilots of 43 Squadron relax off duty, *c.* 1934. They are believed to be inside the Tangmere Hotel. The only pub in the village, it was demolished to make way for wartime runway extensions.

Advertisements for the Tangmere Hotel and Cosy Tea Rooms. The latter are thought to have been situated in an old railway carriage in a hedgerow alongside the Oving Road.

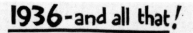

1936-and all that!

Time Marches On—and each year the strain of keeping these drawings clean yet interesting becomes greater— however, as Prof. Brown-Dorf would say, "Honor Virtutis Praemium"

R.A.F. DISPLAY FLASHBACK

"—WHERE'S GEORGE?"

THE NEW SQUADRON CREST

AFTER WE'VE MADE HISTORY WITH THIS NOBLE CREST

THE COLLEGE OF HERALDS TAKE AWAY EVERYTHING BUT ONE SEAX — BUT NEVER MIND, LADS, WE STILL HAVE OUR GOOD NAME AND JOHN ABLITT.

TANGMERE TITTERS

"I DO NOT WISH TO ASSUME COMMAND OF THE AIRCRAFT, SIR!"

THIS YEAR'S STAR TURN, MR. M. (OLD-TIMER) MOORE, WARNS FLT./LT. GIBBON BEFORE TAKING OFF.

NOW THEN, YOU FELLAHS!

FLT./SGT. ('TRAPPER') LAWSON HAD A GOOD CAMP, WITH A BAG OF THIRTY HARES AND FOUR TOP C's

HE CAPS THE LOT!

IN THE FACE OF KEEN COMPETITION L/AC SELLAR WON FIRST PRIZE FOR THE MOST SHAPELESS CAP

THE CRICKET MATCH

OFFICERS XII — 123
AIRMENS XII — 125 for 4

FOUR!

THE C.O., SQDN./LDR. C. GABRIEL FOUND HIS GOLFING EXPERIENCE VERY USEFUL

L/AC TINGLEY GOT TONS AND TONS OF RUNS

P/O G.BUDD PUT IN A BIT OF USEFUL "GROUND TO AIR" FOR THE OFFICERS' XI.

WHAT THE —!

MR. CHARTERS SCORED SEVERAL DIRECT HITS ON BOGNOR PIER.

F/O DOULTON ALL-ROUND ATHLETE, AND THE TALLEST PILOT IN THE SERVICE

STUDY OF FLT/LT ('MIKE') ANDERSON WONDERING IF THEY'LL EVER GET THAT SANGUINARY ENGINE TO START.

GENTLEMEN, PLEASE!

THE LOCAL PUBLICANS FOUND THAT THIS WAS THE ONLY WAY THEY COULD PERSUADE A/G'S TO GO —

WHICH BRINGS ME TO SERGEANTS MITCHENER, CROFTS & KNIGHT, WHO INSPIRED THE SLOGAN 'BEER IS BEST'

—AND TO FINISH OFF, HERE IS L/AC ASH, (OSCAR'), A GREAT WIELDER OF TAIL TROLLEY

AND ONE OF THE SQUADRON'S STALWARTS

BEING THE WORK OF THE OLD MAESTRO E.A.WREN

Tangmere became a regular and popular venue for annual summer camps of the Auxiliary Air Force squadrons, or 'Weekend Airmen' as the regulars called them. Here, cartoonist Chris Wren lampoons the antics and events of 604 Squadron's 1936 camp at Tangmere.

Westland Wapitis of 604 Squadron in formation over Chichester Cathedral during their Tangmere camp, 1936.

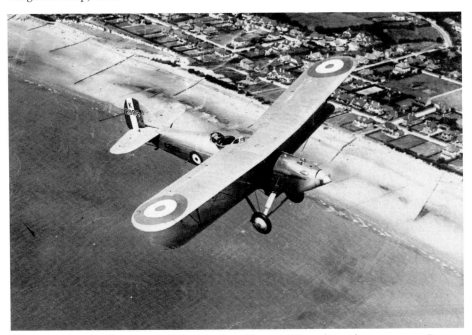

Flt. Lt. 'Jock' Faulds takes his 600 Squadron Hawker Hart along the coast near Bognor Regis during annual camp at Tangmere. Sadly, Faulds was killed shortly afterwards in a civilian air crash at Heston.

A familiar sight over Sussex from Selsey to Rye, the silver Furies from Tangmere were pleasing to the eye, graceful in flight and popular with their pilots. These were the golden days of aviation and Tangmere's halcyon years.

Pilots of 1 Squadron with a Fury, 1936. Note the black armbands being worn in mourning for King George V. During the 1930s, 1 Squadron was famous for formation and tied-together aerobatics, and regularly appeared at the Hendon Air Pageant. Overseas visits to Zurich and Canada were also made, when the squadron was able to wave the flag in its Hawker Fury biplanes.

County of Middlesex (604) Squadron at Tangmere for annual camp, 1935. Unfortunately the scene is tinged with tragedy. On 4 August in this year, one of the squadron's Hawker Demon aircraft, *en route* for Tangmere from its Hendon base, crashed onto the railway line at Collindale. FO Nimmo and his passenger, LAC Mabbutt, were killed.

County of Middlesex (604) Squadron at Tangmere for annual camp, and Tangmere's first glimpse of a Spitfire. On 4 December 1936, test pilot Jeffrey Quill landed prototype K5054 at Tangmere after running short of fuel.

EMPIRE AIR DAY
Saturday, 25th. May 1935.

Royal Air Force Station, Tangmere.

PROGRAMME

of FLYING and

GENERAL *INFORMATION*

Traffic Arrangements.

DEPARTURES. In order to avoid congestion at the exits, cars proceeding to Arundel, Petworth etc., should leave the Aerodrome by the Main Entrance and turn right. Those proceeding to Chichester, Bognor etc., should leave by the South Entrance and left.

◆◆◆◆◆◆◆◆◆◆◆

The Aerodrome will be closed to the public at 7 p.m. when a typhoon will be sounded.

◆◆◆◆◆◆◆◆◆◆◆

Teas and Refreshments will be provided by the Navy, Army and Air Force Institute at popular prices.

◆◆◆◆◆◆◆◆◆◆◆

The public are strictly pohibited from entering the roped off area owing to the danger from aircaft.

◆◆◆◆◆◆◆◆◆◆◆

All proceeds will be devoted to the Royal Air Force Benevolent Fund, with the exception of those in respect of the sale of Air League booklets which are for the benefit of the Air League of the British Empire.

Front cover of the programme for Pre-war Empire Day, 1935. This event was a thrilling spectacle for Britain's air-minded public and attracted large crowds to Tangmere.

A coastal reconnaissance Avro Anson of 217 Squadron at the Empire Air Day display, 29 May 1937. These aircraft shared the pre-war occupancy of RAF Tangmere with the fighters of 1 and 43 Squadrons.

The same schoolboy as above poses alongside a comparatively gargantuan Handley Page Heyford bomber which was visiting the same event at Tangmere.

This Hawker Osprey of the Fleet Air Arm, also visiting for an Empire Air Day in the 1930s, attracts the curiosity of RAF personnel keen to give an unfamiliar type a professional once-over.

A Fairey Hendon bomber of 38 Squadron visits Tangmere, 1937. Quite probably, the event is the annual Empire Air Day display or, possibly, an air defence exercise, as the other aircraft visible are Hawker Hinds of 40 Squadron, also visitors to Tangmere.

A Handley Page Heyford bomber dwarfs the crowd at Tangmere's Empire Air Day, 1937. Notice the two boy scouts being photographed by the troop leader.

This Avro Anson of 217 Squadron overshot on landing at Tangmere, 30 July 1937. It ended up beside the Chichester to Arundel Road. It is hard to believe that this quiet country lane is now the roaring A27 dual carriageway.

This Avro Rota, K4230, '15', of the Royal Aircraft Establishment was an unusual visitor to Tangmere, 1934.

These are the crumpled remains of an Avro Tutor, K6106, of 612 Squadron after it had collided with a Hawker Hector of the same squadron at Tangmere, 26 July 1937.

In February 1937, 72 Squadron formed at Tangmere out of a flight of 1 Squadron to become the first unit in the RAF to operate the Gloster Gladiator biplane fighter. By June of that year the squadron had moved to RAF Church Fenton, Yorkshire.

On 11 February 1939, a Gatwick-based Hawker Audax, K7459, of 19 Elementary & Reserve Flying Training School crashed into a block of flats at Freshfield Road, Brighton, *en route* to Tangmere. The accident, in thick mist, claimed the lives of Sgt. Pilot Brun and the occupants of the flat, twenty-eight-year-old Dorothy Baigent and her two daughters, Audrey, three, and Gwendoline, two. All too soon the loss of military and civilian life through aerial activity would become commonplace.

The Furies of 43 Squadron, airborne for the last time, January 1939. Their drab war-paint of camouflage had been applied during the Munich crisis of 1938 and was in striking contrast to the earlier silver-doped finish.

The pilots of 43 Squadron line up in front of their Hawker Furies at Tangmere, January 1939. This was immediately prior to the squadron's last formation flight with the type before re-equipping with Hawker Hurricanes. With war clouds looming, most of these pilots would later take part in the Battles of France and Britain, many losing their lives.

The First Months of The War, 1939–40

The Hurricanes of 1 Squadron stand on the apron at Tangmere in front of the hangars. Another Hurricane of 43 Squadron commences a low-level pass.

The day war broke out, Sunday 3 September 1939. Airmen hurriedly prepare sandbagged emplacements for Hurricanes of 43 Squadron to protect the aeroplanes from the effects of blast.

An airman of 43 Squadron wearing anti-gas clothing on the same day. No doubt he is anticipating the predicted hordes of German bombers dropping poison gas. Almost a full year was to pass before the Luftwaffe would visit Tangmere.

This airman seems distinctly apprehensive about things as he crouches in an air-raid shelter on the day war was declared.

By contrast, this airman, LAC 'Pompey' Edwards of 43 Squadron, seems positively cheerful about the prospect of war. He is riding the bonnet of a Morris Commercial aircraft refuelling bowser.

This was the Miles Magister communications aircraft of 43 Squadron at Tangmere, 1940. In 1942 an identical aircraft of 1 Squadron spun into the ground at Tangmere, killing PO Sweeting and his civilian passenger, Mr George Martin, whom he had taken for a flight. Martin was the secretary of the Mayor of Brighton. He had been with a civic party entertained in the Officers' Mess to honour the links between Brighton and 1 Squadron, 'Brighton's Own'.

Some of 43 Squadron's pilots alongside Tangmere's hangars, 1940. During the Dunkirk period, the hangars were camouflaged from their pre-war white paint. Note the white bumpers on the pilots cars for extra visibility during the blackout.

The Gloster Gladiators of 605 Squadron, Tangmere, August 1939. The squadron was re-equipped with Hawker Hurricanes by October, but faced the prospect of going to war in this obsolete biplane.

This crumpled wreckage is all that remains from two 605 Squadron Gladiators which collided and crashed near Tangmere, 19 September 1939. FOs Warren and Forbes were killed.

Fairey Battle L7693 was fitted with dual controls and was at Tangmere with 43 Squadron in 1939 to provide Hurricane pilots with night-flying experience.

Snapped illicitly from within the grass at nearby Ford Aerodrome, this Tangmere-based 1 Squadron Hurricane would shortly be winging its way to war in France.

NO. BLANK FIGHTER SQUADRON, R.A.F., SOMEWHERE IN FRANCE: By "MEL"

All these young pilots are fine-looking fellows and as keen as mustard, and they all have, to quote their C.O., " seen the black cross ": in other words, they have engaged the enemy in aerial combat. The R.A.F. nowadays talk about their daily " ten before breakfast," and if we may judge by recent happenings, this is no idle boast. The Air Force has shown that it is as good as ever! This cartoon is the first of a series which our artist has been privileged to do in the actual zone of conflict

Cartoonist 'Mel' caricatured the pilots of 1 Squadron who flew to France from Tangmere, September 1939. Some of those depicted would be among the first 'ace' fighter pilots of the Second World War; others would not return.

The Hurricane of Sqn. Ldr. M.V.M. Clube, CO of 501 Squadron, alongside a wooden flight hut at Tangmere, 1939. The HP42 and Ensign airliners in the background had been pressed into RAF service.

Quicker by rail! Here a Hurricane of 501 Squadron, which had flown out to France from Tangmere in May 1940, begins a return journey for battle damage repairs, courtesy of French Railways.

Newly delivered to 238 Squadron at Tangmere, these Spitfires have national markings applied to their tailfins. 238 Squadron became the first Spitfire squadron based at Tangmere. However, after only one month the aircraft were withdrawn and replaced with Hurricanes, and the squadron was redeployed to RAF Middle Wallop.

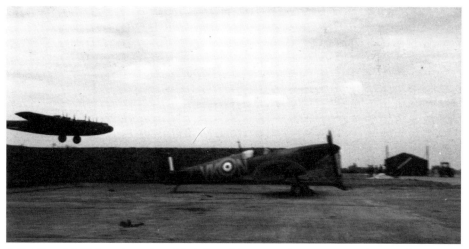

A Spitfire of 238 Squadron, based briefly at Tangmere during May and June of 1940, sits in its blast pen as a four-engined Ensign comes in to land. The Ensign, a civilian airliner pressed into RAF use, was employed transporting men and equipment between England and Europe up until Dunkirk. Thereafter the aeroplane became useful for transporting non-flying squadron personnel between airfields during movements of units.

Hurricane L1867 of 501 Squadron came to grief when it undershot during a night landing at Tangmere, 18 January 1940.

Sqn. Ldr. George Lott led 43 Squadron during 1940 until 9 July when he was hit in an air battle. He was blinded in one eye and was forced to abandon his Hurricane over Fontwell. Out of commission, Lott lost his A1 flying category and could no longer fly 'in action'. He was thus relieved of his command. He also failed to qualify as a Battle of Britain pilot due to an Air Ministry quirk which decreed that the Battle of Britain did not begin until 10 July 1940. Evidently, the Luftwaffe thought otherwise and RAF Fighter Command *knew* otherwise! Nevertheless, rules were rules, and Lott would not qualify for a Battle of Britain clasp to his 1939– 45 Star.

The Battle of Britain, 1940

Three Hurricanes of 601 Squadron are refuelled and re-armed at Tangmere, 1940. Dubbed the 'Millionaires Squadron', the unit's pilots and officers were comprised almost exclusively of upper-class wealthy or titled young men.

One of the first victims of Tangmere-based fighters was this Junkers 87 'Stuka' dive-bomber. It was shot down at St Lawrence, Isle of Wight, on 8 August 1940 by 145 Squadron Hurricanes during an attack on a Channel convoy.

A Hurricane of 145 Squadron, Westhampnett, 1940. Note the one-off bubble cockpit canopy replacing the standard production framed variety usually fitted. Westhampnett, Tangmere's 'satellite' field, is now Goodwood Aerodrome.

Ground personnel of 145 Squadron at Westhampnett. They have a trophy in the form of the swastika-bedecked tailfin of a Heinkel 111. The aeroplane was shot down onto East Beach, Selsey, by squadron pilots on 11 July 1940.

Some of 602 Squadron's groundcrews at Tangmere's satellite field, Westhampnett, August 1940. The squadron operated Spitfires, but home comprised squalid tents, huts, farm buildings and rat-infested farm cottages. Some of the airmen are wearing yellow cloth diamond patches on their uniforms and overalls. During the 1940 invasion scare, this was said to be a means of instant distinction between friend and foe!

Sgt. Pilot Douglas Elcome of 602 Squadron at Westhampnett. Elcome was reported missing in his Spitfire when he failed to return from a patrol on 26 October 1940. No trace of him has ever been found.

Taking off from Tangmere, 20 July 1940. Sgt. Jim Hallowes of 43 Squadron suffered a total engine seizure. He was forced to put down in a field at Amberley, Sussex, causing further damage to the Hurricane, P7384. It was not always just the Luftwaffe who were the enemy!

This Messerschmitt Bf 109 was shot down by Sgt. Mills in a Tangmere-based Hurricane of 43 Squadron in a field beside Shoreham Airport, 13 August 1940. The pilot, Oblt. Paul Temme, was entertained to breakfast by the Army officers who captured him.

FO Bird-Wilson of 17 Squadron had the cockpit door of his Hurricane painted with this distinctive emblem while the squadron was based at Tangmere, August 1940.

Shortly after a ferocious attack by Junkers 87 'Stukas', smoke billows from the burning 43 Squadron hangar, 16 August 1940. At least twelve aircraft were destroyed on the ground and numerous others damaged.

An Army officer watches across the boundary barbed wire as 43 Squadron's hangar goes up in smoke after the 'Stuka' raid. This photograph was taken from approximately where the access road to Tangmere Military Aviation Museum is now situated.

After the smoke has cleared, a Hurricane circles the battered aerodrome, 16 August 1940. The garage hangar with its collapsed roof dominates this depressing scene. Later the collapsed part of the garage hangar was cleared away and the northern part, its open end bricked up, was retained. Among other uses it was, for a time, the station theatre.

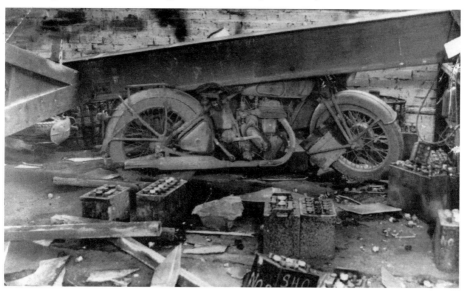

Surrounded by charred batteries, this motorcycle lies crushed beneath a collapsed roof girder. Overall, the scale of damage and desolation was awesome. One young WAAF, emerging from her slit-trench shelter after the raid, remarked, 'Tangmere as we know it has vanished.'

Another view of the terrible damage caused by the 'Stuka' raid, with vehicles in the Motor Transport Section smashed under a collapsed roof. Quite apart from the damage to buildings, equipment and war materials, ten service personnel and three civilians were killed, and a further twenty people seriously injured. Given the scale of the attack, the casualties could have been far higher.

Made in Germany. . . finished in England. One of the Stukas that attacked Tangmere on 16 August 1940 was shot down beside the Selsey road where it attracted much local curiosity.

'He died that England might live.' PO Billy Fiske was an American citizen who volunteered for RAF service and flew Hurricanes with 601 Squadron from Tangmere during the Battle of Britain. On 16 August 1940 he brought his burning Hurricane back to Tangmere after combat, but died from burns and shock the next day.

Billy Fiske, his coffin draped with the Stars and Stripes, is carried to his last resting place at Boxgrove Priory near Tangmere. Fellow RAF officers follow in the funeral procession for this, the first American to be killed in action during the Second World War.

Retribution! Shortly after the horrendous raid by 'Stukas' on 16 August 1940, Sqn. Ldr. Archibald Hope Bt, CO of 601 Squadron, shot down a Messerschmitt 110. The enemy aeroplane crashed into the ornamental pond of Shopwyke House near Tangmere. The event was witnessed by the whole of 601 Squadron – both in the air and on the ground. In this instance, revenge was surely sweet. Later, Shopwyke House was used for accommodation by Tangmere personnel and the pond was converted into a swimming pool.

HRH The Duke of Kent leaves 17 Squadron's Dispersal Hut during a visit to Tangmere, late August 1940. Facing the hut is Station Commander Gp. Capt. J.A. Boret, who allegedly employed captured German aircrews' help to clear up the mess they had created during the bombing of 16 August 1940.

In its howling death dive, a Junkers 87 'Stuka' screams earthwards above the rooftops of Chichester, despatched by fighters from Tangmere on 18 August 1940. The aeroplane crashed in a meadow just off The Broyle.

Sqn. Ldr. George Lott, blinded in one eye on 9 July 1940, visits his squadron at Tangmere's Officers' Mess, 7 September 1940. Within a few hours, two of these pilots would be dead. Flt. Lt. 'Dickie' Reynell and Sqn. Ldr. Ceasar Hull (seated, far right) were both shot down in the same air battle over south London. The Battle of Britain was on with a vengeance.

Pilots of 17 Squadron with a trophy from a Junkers 88 on the wall of their dispersal hut, August 1940. Left to right: S.L. Williams, PO Ross, FO Bird-Wilson.

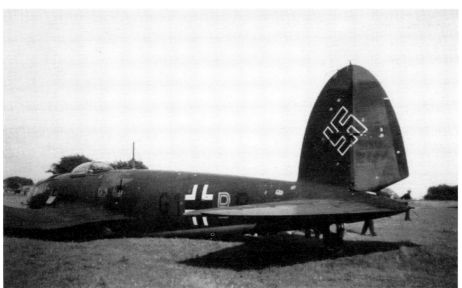

This bullet-holed Heinkel 111 was shot down by Tangmere-based Hurricanes of 43 Squadron, landing beside the River Arun at Wick, 26 August 1940. It was joining a growing tally of victims clawed from the sky over Sussex by Tangmere's relentless defenders.

Lt. zur Karl-Wilhelm Brinkbaumer was a naval officer attached to the Luftwaffe when he was shot down and killed with his Junkers 88 crew near Selsey on 13 August 1940. He is buried in Tangmere churchyard.

THE BRITISH RED CROSS SOCIETY

AND

ORDER OF ST. JOHN

Is forwarding a Photograph of the Grave of

Name *Brinkbäumer*

Rank and Initials *Leutnant W*

Regiment *German Air Force*

Position of Grave *Tangmere Churchyard*

All communications respecting this Photograph should quote the number ....*460*....and be addressed to:—

THE BRITISH RED CROSS SOCIETY

AND

ORDER OF ST. JOHN

7 BELGRAVE SQUARE
LONDON, S.W.

S & D Ltd—15287

This memorial card was sent to Brinkbaumer's family in 1940 via the Red Cross.

Tangmere at War, 1941–44

War is said to be ninety-nine per cent boredom, one per cent excitement. Here, pilots of 616 Squadron fill in the moments of boredom with a card game in one of Tangmere's dispersal huts, 1941.

A Spitfire of 616 Squadron undergoes open-air servicing at Westhampnett, spring 1941. This task was pleasant enough in good weather, but airfields could be bleak, windswept and uncomfortable places for ground crews struggling to get aeroplanes serviceable for operations during inclement weather.

Three Spitfire pilots, Sgts Morton, Brown and Jenks (centre three, left to right), of 616 Squadron with two 'Ops' telephone operators at B Flight Dispersal, Westhampnett, April 1941. The cone-shaped object is a German bomb fin.

What the well-dressed fighter pilot was wearing in 1941. Behind this fearsome spectacle is the visage of Sgt. Pilot Robert Morton, a Spitfire pilot of 616 Squadron, Westhampnett, who was shortly to be shot down over France and taken as a prisoner of war. He displays the flying helmet, goggles and oxygen mask which a fighter pilot had to wear into battle.

FOs Roy Marples (left) and 'Buck' Casson (right) of 616 Squadron act up to the camera at a dance in Brighton's Dome, 28 May 1941. Perhaps the caption should be: 'My goodness, my Guinness!' Casson was shot down over France and taken as a prisoner of war on 9 August 1941. Marples, as a twenty-four-year-old Wing Commander, was killed in a mid-air collision between his Spitfire and another over Washington, West Sussex, on 26 April 1944.

'They also served . . .', or, 'The men who kept 'em flying!' Here, fitter, rigger and armourer pose with 'Buck' Casson's Spitfire. 'They had', recalled Casson, 'got her trimmed to perfection. She was an absolute dream to fly.'

This Spitfire is tucked into its blast pen at Tangmere, April 1941. It was flown by FO 'Buck' Casson and lost on 5 May 1941 when Casson was forced to bale out near Littlehampton following combat damage.

Wg. Cdr. Douglas Bader, the legendary legless fighter pilot, led the Tangmere wing from March 1941 until 9 August of the same year. He was lost over France and taken as a prisoner of war. Here, seated in his Spitfire at Tangmere, he prepares for an offensive patrol over France.

Gp. Capt. Douglas Bader (seated centre, arms folded) with his pilots of the Tangmere Wing, April 1941. At this time the wing was made up of 145, 610 and 616 Squadrons.

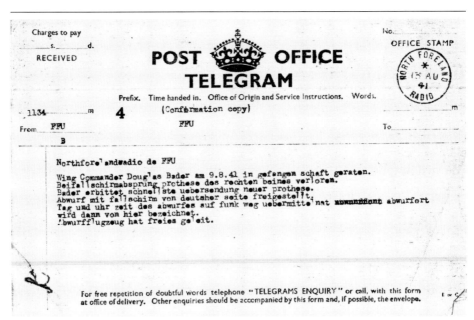

POST OFFICE TELEGRAM

No.

Prefix. Time handed in. Office of Origin and Service Instructions. Words.

(Confirmation copy)

1134   m   **4**   FFU   m

From   FFU

B

To

Northforelandradio de FFU

Wing Commander Douglas Bader am 9.8.41 in gefangen schaft geraten.
Beifallschirmabsprung prothese des rechten beines verloren.
Bader erbittet schnellste uebersendung neuer prothese.
Abwurf mit fallschirm von deutscher seite freigestellt.
Tag und uhr zeit des abwurfes auf funk weg uebermittelnat nxmmmttmmp abwurfert
wird dann von hier bezeichnet.
Abwurfflugzeug hat freies geleit.

The telegram from North Foreland Radio on 13 August 1941, confirming the capture of Wg. Cdr. Douglas Bader. The message went on to say that one of Bader's artificial legs had been lost in his bale-out and stated that an aircraft delivering a replacement would be given safe passage. When this news came, nobody could believe it.

High-speed launch 177 speeds along the Channel. The launch was skippered by Guy Morris (rank unknown) and operated out of Newhaven. Many ditched Tangmere aircrews owed their lives to the RAF Air Sea Rescue launches from Littlehampton and Newhaven.

Capt. Frank Hill of the 31st Fighter Group with his star-spangled Spitfire Vb at Westhampnett, August 1942. This was soon after the arrival of the first American fighter unit. On 19 August that year, the 31st Fighter Group became the first American fighter group in action. Lt. S. Junkin had the distinction of being the first US pilot to score in combat, although he was himself immediately shot down and injured.

Pilots of the 31st Fighter Group, United States Army Air Force, rest on the terrace at Shopwyke House Officers' Mess, summer 1942. Tiredness seems to be in evidence. Could this be combat fatigue, or perhaps nothing more than a post-lunch soporific state?

The Station Padre, Revd Hearn, was a regular and popular visitor to Tangmere and Westhampnett, and a member of the Officers' Mess. He was also the Tangmere Parish Vicar. The 616 Squadron Spitfire in the background is stationary on trestles and not, as it appears, airborne.

Gwendoline Ball, a WAAF from Tangmere, is married to Pte. Charles Nickless, Royal Artillery, 26 May 1941. A WAAF contingent formed the guard of honour. Many of the ceremonies performed by Revd Hearn at Tangmere church during the Second World War were military funerals. Very few weddings took place there. This was a pleasant exception.

This caricature depicts Spitfire Pilot Sgt. Ben Bingley of 616 Squadron, Tangmere. He was killed when his Spitfire crashed in unexplained circumstances on 10 March 1941. Twenty-four-year-old Bingley, a hospital administrator from Leicester, is one of the many RAF casualties buried in Tangmere churchyard.

534 Squadron personnel. From September 1942, this squadron operated at Tangmere with searchlight-equipped 'Turbinlite' Boston IIIs. These were literally flying searchlights designed to illuminate night raiders which, in theory, would then be dealt with by 534 Squadron night-fighter Hurricanes. The scheme was a dismal failure and the squadron disbanded in January 1943. The Havoc aircraft behind was used for training but not fitted with the searchlight. Billy the goat, the squadron's mascot, sits at the feet of the CO, Sqn. Ldr. Kenneth Matthews.

Sgt. Pilot 'Art' Davies, a Hurricane pilot in 534 Squadron at Tangmere, with his wife, 'Lindy'. This picture epitomizes the personal tragedy of war. On 21 October 1942 Davies was killed in a mid-air collision with a Boston of 605 Squadron near the airfield. This picture was taken shortly before his death.

This building in St Pancras, Chichester, was once the Unicorn Pub, a favoured haunt of Tangmere pilots during the war years when publican Arthur King reserved a special welcome for his 'Tangmere boys'. Today, all trace of the building's former use has vanished – the many signatures of wartime fighter pilots on the walls have been obliterated. Who knows what ghosts are there? Sadly, only the doormat inscribed 'UNICORN' survives and may be seen at Tangmere Museum.

Aerial view of RAF Tangmere from 8,300 ft, 17 June 1941. The bombed-out hangars can be seen, as can other evidence of bomb damage, including a string of twelve bomb craters straddling the western end of the main runway. Note that the runways have been painted with camouflage, and the fields and hedges which seem to make up a patchwork effect across the aerodrome itself are also camouflage. The 'hedges' are no more than sprayed tar paint, while different types of grass, etc. have been grown in the various 'fields'. Altogether it was a sophisticated system of disguise, but it is surely arguable as to whether it was really effective.

Spitfire pilots of 129 'Mysore' Squadron wait in readiness in their flying kit, Westhampnett, 1942. Typically, the squadron has a mascot dog.

Station Commander Gp. Capt. C.H. Appleton DSO, DFC (centre), with the Commanders of the five Tangmere squadrons which participated in operations to cover the Dieppe raid of 19 August 1942. The five squadrons, 41, 43, 66, 118 and 501, achieved more than four hundred hours of flying during this one day.

PO Trenchard-Smith from Australia returned to Tangmere in his 43 Squadron cannon-armed Hurricane IIc minus most of his tail section following the Dieppe operation of 19 August 1942. He was instantly named 'Tail-less Ted' the new Antipodean Marsupial! Here he poses at Tangmere with his Hurricane, marked appropriately with an outline map of Australia.

Sgt. Pilot Allan Lee, a nineteen-year-old Spitfire pilot of 501 Squadron, was killed when his Spitfire crashed in bad weather at Billingshurst, returning from the Dieppe raid of 19 August 1942. He was just one of the many RAF casualties laid to rest in Tangmere churchyard during the Second World War.

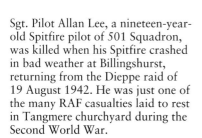

Westergate House. Most of the large houses close to Tangmere were requisitioned for RAF use during the Second World War, including this house which became WAAF living quarters.

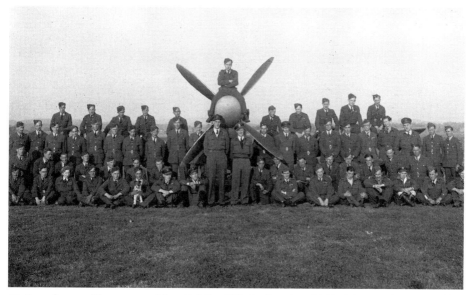

41 Squadron at Tangmere with a Spitfire XII. In October 1943 this squadron moved to Tangmere with its new clipped-wing Spitfire XIIs fitted with the Rolls Royce Griffon engine and extremely fast at low altitudes. On 9 August of the same year, the squadron's Spitfires shot up a railway locomotive and a staff car in France. According to the Tangmere Operations Record Book, 'The occupants, identified as five fat Germans, were reported to have "had it".'

TANGMERE THEATRE

(By kind permission of Officer Commanding)

presents

'FLARE PATH'

BY

F/Lt. TERENCE RATTIGAN

Directed by

ANTHONY ASQUITH

With the Full West End Cast from
The Apollo Theatre, London

Sunday, May 23rd, 1943

Terrence Rattigan's play, *Flare Path*, was performed at Tangmere on 23 May 1943. The cast for this production included a very young George Cole as Percy. Other West End shows came to Tangmere, including the entire company of the Windmill Theatre. Performers included Noel Coward, Vera Lynn and music hall duo, Gert & Daisy.

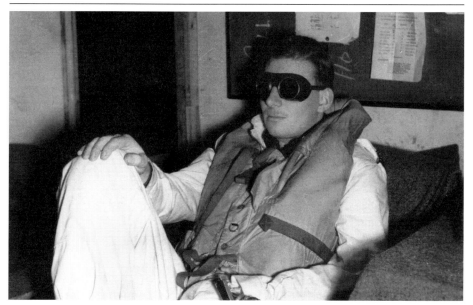

Sqn. Ldr. James MacLachlan DSO, DFC led 1 Squadron at Tangmere during 1941 and 1942 on night intruder operations. Having lost his left arm in action over Malta in February 1941, he had an artificial limb fitted with special attachments for operating a Hurricane's controls. Here MacLachlan is waiting for night operations wearing night vision acclimatization goggles. He was killed in a daylight operation over France on 29 June 1943.

Another amazingly successful night fighter and intruder pilot in 1 Squadron at this time was a Czech, FO Karel Kuttelwascher. 'Kut', as he was known, flew numerous night sorties from Tangmere, claiming many German aircraft. He died of a heart attack in 1959.

Tangmere Cottage opposite the camp's main gates became the secret local operations centre for 161 (Special Duties) Squadron. From here, agents awaited transit to France via the squadron's Lysander aircraft during moonlight operations into German-occupied territory.

The 'Operations Room', Tangmere Cottage. One wonders what the brown paper parcel on the mantelshelf contains. Quite probably it is some highly secret package awaiting carriage to France that night. Today, Tangmere Cottage is a private home.

A group of 161 Squadron Lysander pilots with one of their aeroplanes at Tangmere, 1943. Left to right: FO McCairns, Flt. Lt. Verity, Gp. Capt. Pickard, Flt. Lt. Vaughan-Fowler, FO Rymills. The squadron dogs are Ming and Henry.

This cartoon was drawn by one of the agents taken into France by a Lysander from Tangmere. It advises: 'To avoid a rugby scrum, separate those arriving and departing!'

Sqn. Ldr. Stephen Hankey was a Special Duties Lysander pilot with 161 Squadron. He was killed when he crashed, returning to Tangmere in fog on the night of 16/17 December 1943. The two agents with him also perished.

Gp. Capt. Ron Hockey of 138 (Special Duties) Squadron in the cockpit of his Halifax with his personal emblem beneath the cockpit. Hockey flew out of Tangmere in a Halifax bomber on the night of 28 December 1941 to parachute agents, Jozef Gabcik and Jan Kubis, into Czechoslovakia for the assassination of SS Gauleiter Reinhard Heydrich. The mission ultimately led to the reprisal destruction of two Czech villages and their populations at Lidice and Lezaky.

A Typhoon of 486 Squadron, airborne from Tangmere, shows off its ruggedly purposeful lines over the Sussex countryside, 1943.

A 181 Squadron Typhoon is 'bombed-up' at Tangmere, June 1943.

Wg. Cdr. Desmond Scott, RNZAF, with his Typhoon, late 1943. At this time, Scott was leading the Tangmere Wing and had his initials, DJS, on the fuselage of his aeroplane. This particular Typhoon was the first in service with a modified sliding 'bubble' cockpit canopy. Perched on the tail is Scott's dog, Kim.

Flt. Lt. Charles Brayshaw DFC, with his Typhoon at Merston. Brayshaw was lost in a Typhoon of 247 Squadron flying from the Tangmere satellite of Merston on 21 February 1944. His aircraft, hit by flak, crashed into the sea ten miles off Cabourg.

Pilots of 197 Squadron with a Typhoon, 1943. Four of these pilots were later killed. Notes the unusual car-door type entry into the cockpit.

These Typhoon pilots of 197 Squadron are larking around on bicycles behind their dispersal hut at Tangmere, 1943. Standard individual means of transport around the station was by means of bicycle.

Two New Zealand Typhoon pilots of 486 Squadron at Tangmere, Frank Murphy (left) and Allan Smith (right), sharing a joke, January 1943. Together, these pilots were successfully scrambled from Tangmere on 29 April 1943, and shot down a pair of Messerschmitt 109s into the English Channel.

Pilots and personnel of 486 Squadron, A Flight, outside their dispersal hut at Tangmere, 1943. In the background, one of the squadron Typhoons pokes its nose from its blast pen.

Tangmere bound . . . but at Brighton found! This Typhoon, JP677, of 168 Squadron was escorting a VIP Hudson from Europe to Tangmere when it hit Brighton's West Pier and crashed onto the beach, 26 November 1944.

FO J.S. Hamilton of Canada with his Spitfire IX of 412 Squadron at Tangmere, May 1944.

The Officers' Mess at Tangmere, 21 April 1944. On this occasion the Supreme Allied Commander, Gen. Dwight D. Eisenhower, dined with his senior air commanders during the prelude to 'Overlord', or D-Day, on 6 June 1944. Eisenhower (rear left) is in earnest conversation with Air Chief Marshal Sir Trafford Leigh-Mallory.

Gen. Eisenhower prepares to depart from Tangmere in his personal C-47 Dakota transport, 21 April 1944. Note the Stars and Stripes flying in front of the cockpit.

Supreme Headquarters
ALLIED EXPEDITIONARY FORCE
Office of the Supreme Commander

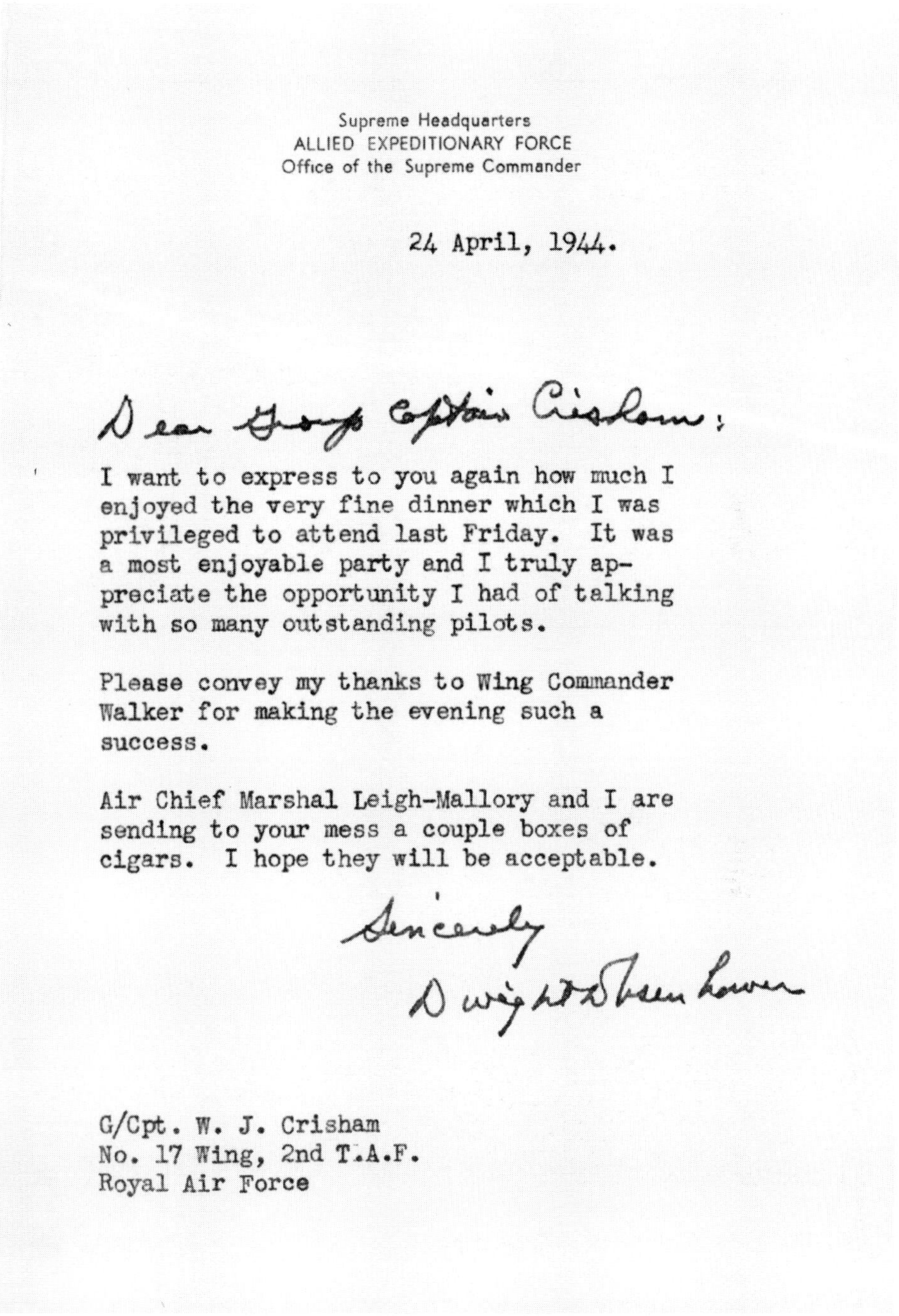

24 April, 1944.

Dear Group Captain Crisham:

I want to express to you again how much I enjoyed the very fine dinner which I was privileged to attend last Friday. It was a most enjoyable party and I truly appreciate the opportunity I had of talking with so many outstanding pilots.

Please convey my thanks to Wing Commander Walker for making the evening such a success.

Air Chief Marshal Leigh-Mallory and I are sending to your mess a couple boxes of cigars. I hope they will be acceptable.

Sincerely
Dwight D. Eisenhower

G/Cpt. W. J. Crisham
No. 17 Wing, 2nd T.A.F.
Royal Air Force

The letter of thanks sent by Gen. Eisenhower following his lunch in Tangmere Officers' Mess, 21 April 1944.

Soon after D-Day and the establishment of forward airfields in France, beer was delivered to the troops there by way of drop tanks slung beneath Spitfires. Here, a Norwegian pilot watches from the wing of his Spitfire IX as beer is transferred from kegs to a tank. Previously described as at Tangmere, this is more likely to have been at one of Tangmere's satellites: Selsey, Funtington, Bognor, Appledram, Westhampnett or Merston.

Sqn. Ldr. N.R. Fowlow, CO of 411 'Grizzly Bear' Squadron, RCAF, walks to his Spitfire at Tangmere, May 1944. His flying kit, parachute, etc. are slung over his shoulder. A cricket match is in progress in the background. Fowlow was killed in a collision with another Spitfire over Normandy on 12 June 1944.

Special tactical recognition markings in the form of black and white stripes are applied to a 'Grizzly Bear' Squadron Spitfire of the RCAF at Tangmere, 5 June 1944 (the eve of D-Day).

King George VI and Queen Elizabeth visit RAF Tangmere for an investiture, 14 July 1944. Here they are outside the Officers' Mess with senior officers.

Gp. Officer Balfour proudly shows His Majesty the Tangmere WAAF contingent, lined up for inspection during the Tangmere Investiture, 14 July 1944.

His Majesty pins a medal on the chest of one of the RAF officers decorated at the Tangmere Investiture, 14 July 1944.

Two Canadian Spitfire pilots of 127 Wing wrestle with the delights of life under canvas, May 1944. With so many squadrons and men crammed into Tangmere and its satellites during the run-up to D-Day, not all could be housed under cover. Very soon the wing would move to France, where these primitive living conditions were to be replicated.

Magazines and cigarettes are sorted at Tangmere for distribution to the personnel of 127 Wing, RCAF, May 1944. The wing comprised six Canadian Spitfire squadrons: 401, 403, 411, 412, 416 and 421.

This USAF Mosquito of the 654 Bomb Squadron, 25 Bomb Group, diverted to Tangmere, damaged by flak and hampered by fog after a reconnaissance mission over Arnhem, 22 September 1944. Bob Walker (left) was the pilot and Roy Conyers (right) the navigator. After repairs at Tangmere, Walker air tested his Mosquito and unofficially took a young WAAF on her first flight. The WAAF in question had steered Walker and Conyers to Tangmere after they radioed Mayday.

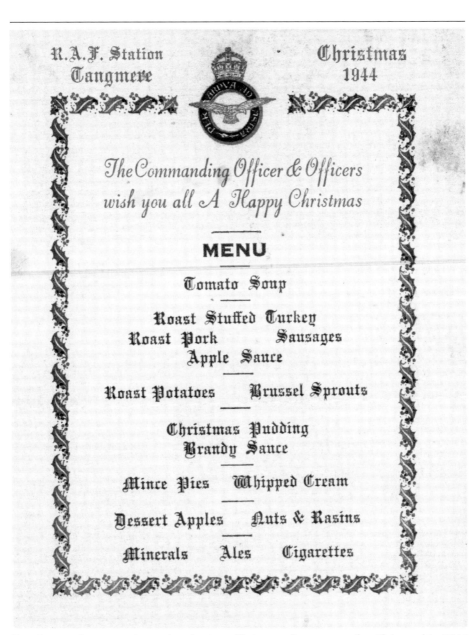

R.A.F. Station
Tangmere

Christmas
1944

The Commanding Officer & Officers
wish you all A Happy Christmas

MENU

Tomato Soup

Roast Stuffed Turkey
Roast Pork   Sausages
Apple Sauce

Roast Potatoes   Brussel Sprouts

Christmas Pudding
Brandy Sauce

Mince Pies   Whipped Cream

Dessert Apples   Nuts & Rasins

Minerals   Ales   Cigarettes

Despite wartime austerity and rationing, Christmas fare seems plentiful on this 1944 menu. By tradition, officers waited on the other ranks for Christmas dinner.

SECTION SIX

The Post-war Era, 1945–69

Some controversy surrounds the age of Tangmere's control tower, but this photograph is believed to date from 1945. In any case, the tower was built either very late in the war or just offer it. Before this, flying control was conducted in a rudimentary fashion from a hut or runway controller's caravan – Air Traffic Control was a much later science. The number 25 indicates the runway currently in use.

The Fighter Leaders School came to Tangmere, 1945. Here, pilots are on the first course. Seated (centre front) is Gp. Capt. Douglas Bader, returning to Tangmere after four years incarceration as a prisoner of war. Some of that time he spent in the notorious Colditz Castle.

Spitfire 21s of 1 Squadron drawn up in the standard tail-to-tail 'pose', with pilots and ground crew, 1946. Very soon the squadron would enter the jet age with Meteors.

A semi-derelict Junkers 88-G at Tangmere, 1947. Here, it had been used by the Enemy Aircraft Flight, Central Fighter Establishment, after being captured intact in 1945. Flown in RAF markings, the aeroplane was alloted RAF serial number VK888. This is roughly where the Tangmere Military Aviation Museum now stands.

This battered hulk is the remains of a Fiat G-55 of the Italian Air Force which came to the Enemy Aircraft Flight at Tangmere in 1945. It ended its days in a field across the road from the main aerodrome, roughly opposite the present site of the Tangmere Military Aviation Museum. Tangmere parish church can be seen beyond the tail fin.

A Meteor F4, EE549, at Tangmere, 1946. This aircraft was to become one of the three Meteors taken over by the High Speed Flight. In it, Gp. Cpt. E.M. Donaldson broke the World Air Speed Record at 616 mph off the Sussex coast. The aeroplane is now preserved at Tangmere Military Aviation Museum.

Gp. Capt. E.M. 'Teddy' Donaldson (right) supervises as the record-breaking Meteor is towed out at Tangmere. Latterly, Donaldson (by then an Air Commodore) was Air Correspondent for the *Daily Telegraph*. He died in 1992 and is buried in Tangmere churchyard.

A 1 Squadron Harvard above the south-eastern boundary of RAF Tangmere. In August 1947, 1 Squadron suffered the indignity of losing its frontline Meteor fighters and being relegated to an Instrument Flying Training Unit equipped with Harvards and Oxfords. This lamentable period lasted about a year before the squadron was re-issued with Meteors.

This was the disastrous result of brake failure in a Mosquito, RL198, which ran into the parked RAF Kenley Station Flight Anson, NK235, at Tangmere, 21 April 1947.

'Flame Out' was the name on this visiting USAF Shooting Star which brought some colour to an austere post-war Tangmere, 1948. The name is a colloquial term given to jet engine failure.

A group of pilots from 222 Squadron with a Meteor F3 at Tangmere, 1948. The squadron formed part of the Tangmere wing at this time.

Meteors of 1 and 222 Squadrons of the Tangmere wing wait to take off for an air exercise over the Isle of Wight, 15 April 1948. However, even as early as the end of the 1940s, Tangmere's geographical location was starting to make the station irrelevant in the air defence of the UK. With the Cold War the threat now came from the East, across the North Sea. Air battles over the Isle of Wight were history and no longer a likely or planned-for scenario. Britain's future air defence would be concentrated along its northern and eastern coasts.

Annual summer camp of 611 Squadron, 1948. Spitfire FR14, MV309, of 611 Squadron, Royal Auxiliary Air Force, taxies past squadron pilots who are busy examining hits on an air-towed target drogue.

'Battle of Britain' Class locomotive, 34067, named in honour of RAF Tangmere in common with several other famous Battle of Britain stations, 1947. Fortunately this locomotive survived the scrapman's cutter and is currently preserved by the Mid-Hants Railway.

Looking towards 1 Squadron dispersal and Tangmere village, winter 1948. The tarmac apron, already much widened since pre-war days, was later to be extended yet further into a massive concrete pan to facilitate better operation and movement of jet aircraft.

An unusual visitor to Tangmere in 1949 was the French Air Force Junkers 52 tri-motor transport aircraft.

An Airspeed Oxford of the Instrument Training Squadron, Tangmere, about to touch down, summer 1949.

The crimson Meteor T7 two-seat jet trainer prototype at Tangmere, after a 5,000 mile European sales trip, June 1948. This private venture aeroplane carried the civilian registration G-AKPK.

This all-silver Sea Mosquito of the Royal Navy found a temporary home at Tangmere in August 1948, when nearby Royal Naval Air Station Ford (HMS *Peregrine*) was temporarily closed for a refurbishment programme which included runway resurfacing.

Situated on The Trundle, Goodwood, these three radio receiver masts were part of RAF Station Tangmere, where a round-the-clock signals watch system was operated.

The radio receiver room on The Trundle with its state-of-the-art technology, summer 1948.

'Next Objective' is the racy nose art on this visiting USAF B-29 Superfortress at Tangmere, 1949. The aircraft was probably participating in 'Foil', a major UK air defence exercise.

A civilian Vickers Viking airliner, G-AJJN, a visitor to Tangmere after being diverted from its intended destination by bad weather, late 1940s.

Meteors of 1 Squadron taxi out for take-off and pass between the hangars and control tower. Ground crews wheel away the starting equipment.

Two Meteor F4s of 43 Squadron scorch down Tangmere's main runway during a scramble, summer 1949. For almost twenty years the sight and sound of the ubiquitous 'Meatbox' would be familiar in and around Tangmere.

Flight Commanders and senior pilots of 43 Squadron outside their dispersal hut, 1950. At this time, Sqn. Ldr. H.R. 'Dizzy' Allen (centre) led this squadron in Meteors.

The badge of 43 Squadron incorporated a fighting cock, so it is natural that its members should have been known through their history as 'The Fighting Cocks'. Here, Cocky the mascot sits proudly on the canopy of the CO's Meteor at Tangmere, giving a new dimension to that part of an aeroplane known as the cockpit! The squadron's rival, 1 Squadron, rather unkindly named them the 'Sussex Chicken Farmers'.

The engines of a 43 Squadron Meteor F4 are run up in one of the wartime blast pens at Tangmere, 1950. The wire cage across the air intake was to prevent ground staff being sucked into the Rolls Royce Derwent engines, such situations not being conducive to good morale among airmen!

The Meteor F4 aerobatic team of 43 Squadron over Sussex, 1950. At this time the wartime practice of marking aircraft with squadron-identifying code letters was still being continued. The colourful pre-war squadron markings reappeared later that summer.

Sgt. Pilot Crippen DFM was a much feared mascot on the station during the late 1940s and early '50s. Crippen, who had his own chair in the Sergeants' Mess, appears in many photographs of the period at Tangmere. He was held in greater dread than the station warrant officer!

This 540 Squadron Mosquito PR 34, VL625, belly landed at Tangmere after a fire warning light showed, 21 August 1950. Smashing its perspex nose and shearing its port propeller, the wooden aircraft skidded to a halt but did not ignite. Either a faulty light had lit up, or the precautionary post-crash dousing of foam prevented an inferno.

Four Meteors of 1 Squadron fly over a parked squadron aeroplane as they perform an aerobatic 'Flying One' routine at Tangmere, early 1950.

A 'Flying One' routine ended in tragedy, 19 April 1950. The formation leader, Flt. Lt. P.W. Speller, was killed after the No. 2 aeroplane cut the tail off his Meteor. The inverted wreckage of Speller's aeroplane fell close to the control tower and burnt out.

Gp. Capt. G. Manton (left) in conversation with Sqn. Ldr. H.R. 'Dizzy' Allen (centre) and the Padre, Revd D.J.C. Hearn (right), at an RAF Ball in the Officers' Mess at Tangmere, 1950.

Somehow this car found its way onto the stage in the Officers' Mess at Tangmere during a Mess Night, 1950. High jinks and boisterous behaviour in RAF messes became almost a wartime tradition, but behaviour became a little more staid and respectable post-war.

A B-17 Flying Fortress of the US Navy visiting Tangmere, early 1950s. On numerous occasions between 1942 and 1944, B-17s of the US 8th Air Force landed at Tangmere with battle damage, low on fuel or with dead and dying crew following daylight raids into occupied Europe. On 5 November 1943 a crippled Thorpe Abbots-based B-17X landed with only the pilot and co-pilot on board. The rest of the crew had baled out over Germany.

The ubiquitous Tiger Moth, which was still in use for training and communications work, c. 1954. These aeroplanes were visiting to give ATC cadets air experience flights. In the background are the modern Meteor NF11 jet fighters of 29 Squadron.

Personnel of 1 Squadron with their Meteor F8s at Tangmere, 1952. At this time the squadron was led by Sqn. Ldr. J.L.W. Ellacombe DFC. Tail-to-tail pictures of 1 Squadron aeroplanes had become a well-established tradition.

FO Mike Chandler of Tangmere's 1 Squadron participated in the 1952 King's Cup and South Coast air races in this Miles Hawk, G-ADWT. Tangmere was its temporary home.

Radio test bench in 1 Squadron's radio workshop, May 1952. It is thought this picture was taken in what is now the Tangmere Military Aviation Museum.

Air Vice Marshal Sir Charles Longcroft presents 1 Squadron with its standard, 24 April 1953. It was a proud moment for the unit, the first RAF squadron to be presented with a standard. Appropriately, its motto was *In Omnibus Princeps* – 'First in all things'.

The newly presented 1 Squadron standard is dipped in salute as it is marched past the squadron by FO Mike Chandler. Note the recently extended concrete apron.

The Tangmere Station badge, with the motto 'Attack to Defend', was finally awarded in 1953. Contrary to popular belief, the badge did not exist before this date.

This crowded car park is indicative of public interest at the Battle of Britain display at Tangmere, 1953. Forty years on and the cars of the period, as much as the aeroplanes, are collectors' items.

The Hawker Hunter prototype, WB188, is prepared for an attempt on the World Air Speed Record at Tangmere, September 1953. This historic aeroplane is now preserved at the Tangmere Military Aviation Museum.

Sqn. Ldr. Neville Duke makes a triumphant return to Tangmere, 7 September 1953. He had broken the World Air Speed Record off the Sussex coast at Littlehampton at 727.63 mph, in the all-red Hawker Hunter prototype, WB188.

An armourer feeds ammunition into the starboard 20 mm wing cannons of a 29 Squadron Meteor NF11 at Tangmere, 24 February 1952. In the post-war years of its life as a fighter station, a night-fighter squadron was maintained at Tangmere in addition to the day-fighter squadrons. Between 1950 and 1957, 29 Squadron fulfilled this role.

This Meteor NF11, WD603, of 29 Squadron ditched in the sea off Littlehampton after a navigational error resulted in the aeroplane running out of fuel, 20 October 1953. FO Sneddon and PO Sweetman were rescued unhurt by a Royal Navy Dragonfly helicopter from Ford.

A Ford-based Dragonfly, of the type that rescued Sneddon and Sweetman, pays a visit to Tangmere.

The armourers of 1 and 29 Squadrons during work on a well-stripped Meteor F8 of 1 Squadron at Tangmere, 1954. Note the armament of four nose-mounted 20 mm cannons.

A Meteor NF11 and a Hawker Hunter in formation over Chichester Cathedral. This picture was used on a Tangmere Christmas card of the 1950s and makes an interesting comparison with the photograph of Wapitis over the city (p. 38). It is almost impossible to comprehend that a timespan of less than twenty years separates the two pictures. Such was the pace of aeronautical development that the aircraft types seem worlds apart.

A Supermarine Swift of 56 Squadron visits Tangmere, 1954. As usual, visiting aircraft types, if they were new or unusual, attracted a good deal of attention from station personnel. Sadly, the Swift was never a success and did not live up to the superlative Supermarine name.

A visiting Vampire FB5 is framed by the tail of a Meteor F8 bearing the letters JAK. These were the initials of the station commander between March 1953 and November 1955, Gp. Capt. John Alexander Kent. The aeroplane was his personal machine – such was the privilege of rank.

A DH Comet 2 airliner, XK670, on the concrete apron at Tangmere following a bad weather diversion, 1950s. This was one of several operated by RAF Transport Command for transport purposes.

A civilian Tipsy-B, owned and flown from Tangmere by Mrs Gordon Slade, 10 May 1950. Exactly why it was being operated from Tangmere is a little obscure, as the station was entirely military. However, it makes an interesting and pleasing variation from the usual service hardware.

Hunter F5s in the servicing hangar with 34 Squadron's distinctive and colourful markings. In October 1955 the squadron re-equipped with Hunter F5s at Tangmere. One year later the squadron redeployed to Cyprus and flew fighter cover missions during the Suez operation.

RAF Tangmere's Station Flight Avro Anson T20, VS529, in its hangar at Tangmere, c. 1956. The name 'TANGMERE' is painted behind the cockpit.

By May 1957, 'Faithful Annie's' days were done. She ended her life in this sad state on the Tangmere fire dump for use in crash rescue training.

Visiting Gloster Javelin fighters of 23, 46 and 141 Squadrons, 1957. They were temporarily based here as an operating station for participation in the Farnborough Air Show.

An interesting view of Tangmere through the landing-wheel doors of one of the parked Javelins, as three more Javelins make a low pass in line astern. The 'Flying Flat Iron' was the unkind nickname for this less than successful design.

This motley collection of motor transport has the appearance of a travellers' encampment. It is, in fact, the mobile Ground Controlled Approach System alongside runway 25/07, 1954.

The annual inspection of the Commander-in-Chief, Fighter Command, at RAF Tangmere, 1959. The commander marches in through the main gate accompanied by his staff officers. In the background is Tangmere Cottage with its convenient proximity to the aerodrome's main gate.

The ever-ready fire and crash crews at Tangmere, April 1960. These were often called upon to deal with aircraft emergencies on and around the aerodrome, particularly during the station's period as a UK Master Diversion Airfield.

One emergency tackled by Tangmere's fire crews involved this star-spangled Voodoo of 81st Tactical Fighter Wing, USAF, which made a spectacular emergency landing, 11 April 1962. Hitting the slight gradient of runway 25 too fast, both main wheels sheared, with one ending up by Oving church, the other on the concrete apron by the hangars.

Speed of another kind came to Tangmere in the form of Donald Campbell's *Bluebird*, 1962. Campbell stands on the left as his car is prepared for trials along the runways at Tangmere.

The engines of *Bluebird* roar into life before she is put through her paces. For these test runs the wheel side-covers have not been fitted, presumably to allow quick and unhindered access to the wheels.

HRH Princess Alexandra is greeted by the Duke of Norfolk (left) and the station commander as she arrives at RAF Tangmere in an aircraft of the Queen's Flight, 1964.

This odd-looking contraption was a Bensen B-7MC gyrocopter and appeared at one of the Tangmere Battle of Britain 'At Home' days, 1960s. The aeroplane, registered G-APUD, is now preserved and on display at Greater Manchester Museum of Science & Industry.

'At Home' display at Tangmere, 14 September 1963. These displays marked the anniversary of the Battle of Britain.

Vickers Varsities of 115 Squadron lined up on the concrete apron at Tangmere, 1961. A 22 Squadron Search and Rescue Whirlwind helicopter is in the foreground. By this time the days of resident squadrons at Tangmere were drawing to a close.

FOR SALE

By Private Arrangement

A DELIGHTFULLY SITUATED

500 Acre ESTATE

A CONVENIENTLY-SIZED RESIDENCE
with
NUMEROUS TIED COTTAGES

Buildings and Outhouses in
Excellent Condition

GARAGE FACILITIES for 1,000 Cars

Would suit gentleman with 1,000 Cars

Nearest Railway Station 3 miles

May be viewed by Appointment on

13th, 14th, 15th August, 1963

Tongue-in-cheek, Tangmere Station personnel produced this handbill when the last flying squadrons, 115 and 245, moved out. In fact, the station remained open for another seven years.

Spitfire TE311 proudly stood at Tangmere's main gate until closure in 1970. Its departure almost met with more local sadness than the closure of the station itself.

Mike Rondot's artist's impression catches the infamous moment when Flt. Lt. 'Al' Pollock, airborne from Tangmere, flew his Hawker Hunter under the top span of Tower Bridge, 4 April 1968. This was during the last fighter sortie flown from the airfield.

A 242 Operational Conversion Unit C-130 Hercules from nearby RAF Thorney Island lets go a parachute supply drop over Tangmere, 1969.

Studied concentration on the faces of the flight-deck crew on board a Thorney Island-based C-130 Hercules of 242 Operational Conversion Unit as it approaches Tangmere for a practice parachute supply drop, early 1970s.

Air Marshal Sir Leslie Mavor, Air Officer Commanding Training Command, presents the preliminary flying badge to HRH Prince Charles at Tangmere, 2 August 1969. HRH Prince Charles had completed eighty hours of flying on the Queen's Flight Chipmunk.

The last flying unit based at Tangmere was 623 Gliding School which remained operational at the airfield until June 1975. Here, one of the school's Slingsby T-21 B gliders passes over the eastern boundary. The solitary T2 hangar was a post-war addition, as were the large concrete blast walls designed to protect the station's Meteors from air attack as they were parked on their Operational Readiness Platforms.

Closure and Decline, 1970–92

An oblique aerial shot, looking from the north, after Tangmere Station's closure, late 1970s. Note the runways, perimeter tracks, dispersals, hangars and buildings. The outline of the pre-war landing circle can also be seen. Much of the housing development comprises airmen's and officers' married quarters. The main A27 road runs across the bottom left corner.

At the ceremony to mark the closure of RAF Tangmere, the scroll presented to the station to mark the granting of the Honorary Freedom of the City of Chichester is paraded before return to the Mayor of Chichester for safe keeping, 16 October 1970. The scroll has now returned to Tangmere and is at the Tangmere Military Aviation Museum.

The Mayor of Chichester receives back the Freedom Scroll, 16 October 1970.

The closure ceremony as personnel march off the parade ground for the very last time, 16 October 1970. The NAAFI building is that seen on p. 22.

By the late 1970s the air of neglect across the station was turning to decay and dilapidation. These are the T2 hangars which were shortly to be renovated, converted for grain storage and put into use by the EEC Agricultural Intervention Board. The flight huts have all vanished with only the concrete bases remaining.

Where fighter pilots had once raced to waiting Spitfires and Hurricanes, police motorcyclists undergo instruction on the perimeter track at Tangmere, 1979. The huge concrete blast walls to protect post-war jet fighters can be seen in the background.

The main gate to the camp, which had seen history in the making and through which some of the finest men and women in the Service had come and gone, was soon swept away by residential development. A new road called Chichester Drive and an adjacent new business park unimaginatively named City Fields serve to illustrate how quickly and carelessly history and heritage are cast aside and forgotten. Fortunately, the station sign is now preserved in Tangmere Military Aviation Museum.

Once spick and span, the guardroom begins to get a little shabby around the edges. The station warrant officer would have had apoplexy!

The once opulent splendour of the Officers' Mess begins to fall into decline after closure of Tangmere as an RAF station, October 1970. The station commander would not have approved.

Wrecked cars litter what had been the fuel dump as dereliction sets in, 1970s. The station motor transport officer would have been distinctly unimpressed.

THIS STONE
ERECTED BY LOCAL SUBSCRIPTION
IN 1976 COMMEMORATES

TANGMERE AIRFIELD

FAMOUS IN TWO WORLD WARS
AND IN the FOREFRONT of
the BATTLE of BRITAIN 1940

IT WAS MANNED BY
ROYAL AIR FORCE SQUADRONS
WHOSE VALIANT MEMORY
IS RECORDED FOR ALL TO SEE AT THE
CHURCH of ST ANDREW TANGMERE

Gp. Capt. Douglas Bader CBE, DSO, DFC unveiled this memorial stone on the green at the end of Church Lane in Tangmere village, 18 December 1976. It is a fitting local tribute to the sacrifices made by the men and women of RAF Tangmere.

Acknowledgements

In submitting this I would like to thank all those who have helped with photographs and information . I have endeavoured to thank everyone but apologize for any ommisions I may have made.

Wg. Cdr. H.R. Allen • P. Arnold • Gp. Capt. D. Bader • J. Beedle • Air Vice Marshall H.A.C. Bird-Wilson • R. Bonser • British Rail • Sqn. Ldr. L.H. Casson • Chichester Observer • Air Commodore R.A. Chisholm • E. Coates R. Darlington • Gp. Capt. W.D. David • P. Dimond • Air Commodore E.M. Donaldson • Sqn. Ldr. N. Duke • Flight • P.G. Foote • Fox Photos • A. Fraser Wg. Cdr. A. Grant • G. Hazel • L.F. Hewstock • Imperial War Museum K. King • J. Kyle • R. Lake • E. Marsden • Ministry of Defence • G. Patmore M. Payne • F. Prebble • RAF Museum • G. Ramsey • W.G. Ramsay Dr Rauchle • RCAF • K. Rimmel • S. Sampson • B. J. Scandrett • M. Shaw G.F. Simmons • Tangmere Aviation Museum • C. Thomas • Topix Gp. Capt. H. Verity • Col. R. Walker, USAF • E. K. Watson • N.M. Woodall

In addition, special thanks to Julie for her help, support and understanding during the preparation of this book.